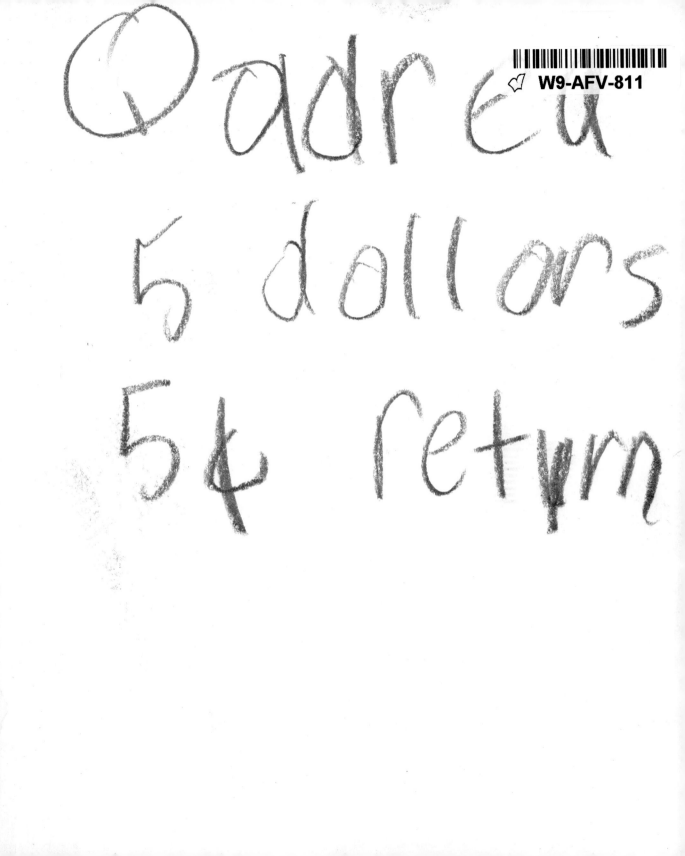

Oadreu

5 dollars

5¢ return

Long Walk to School

A Story About Bullying

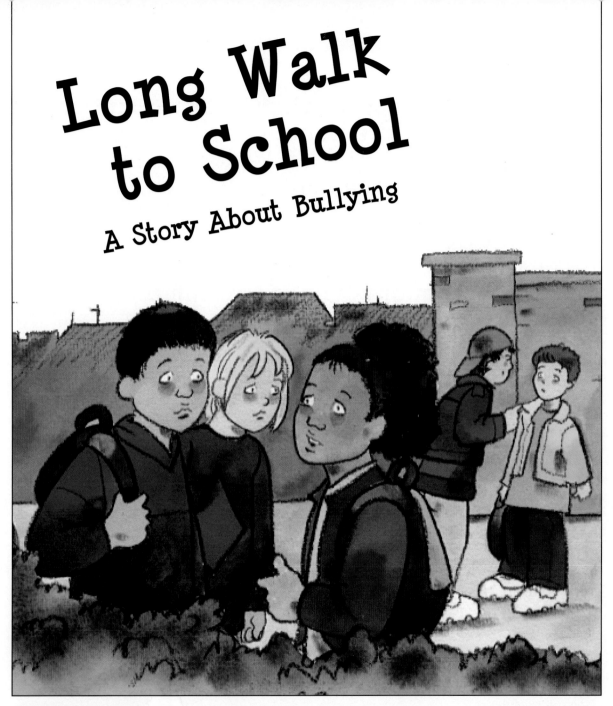

Written by
Cindy Leaney

Illustrated by
Peter Wilks

Rourke
Publishing LLC
Vero Beach, Florida 32964

Before you read this story, take a look at the front cover of the book. On their way to school, José, Emily, and Makayla see something they don't like.

1. What do you think is happening?

2. And how might bullying become part of the story?

Produced by SGA Illustration and Design
Designed by Phil Kay
Series Editor: Frank Sloan

www.rourkepublishing.com

Library of Congress Cataloging-in-Publication Data

Leaney, Cindy.
   Long walk to school : safety outdoors / by Cindy Leaney ; illustrated by Peter Wilks.
     p. cm. -- (Hero club safety)
   Summary: The Hero kids help a boy who is being bullied, as well as the one doing the bullying.
   ISBN 1-58952-745-3
   1. Bullying--Juvenile literature. [1. Bullying. 2. Bullies. 3. Safety.] I. Wilks, Peter, ill. II. Title. III. Series: Leaney, Cindy. Hero club safety.

BF637.B85L43 2003
371.5'8--dc21

2003000232

Printed in the USA
MP/W

Welcome to The Hero Club!
Read about all the things that happen to them.
Try and guess what they'll do next.

www.theheroclub.com

"Ha! You think you're so smart. You think you're better than everybody else just because you get good grades."

"That kid is bullying him."

"What should we do?"

"Let's just wait a minute and listen."

"Yeah, you're just teacher's pet. You always know the answers."

8

"What's in the bag? Is this
   your lunch?"

"It's mine."

"Give him his lunch back."

11

"Why should I?"

"Because it's his lunch."

"What if I don't?"

13

"We'll tell Mrs. Hampton and you'll be in trouble."

"Big deal. I'm always in trouble.
Who cares?"

"You should care."

"You should work harder instead of bullying the kids who do."

"Then you wouldn't be in trouble all the time."

"It wouldn't make any difference. The teachers hate me."

18

"No they don't. Give him his lunch or we'll all be late for school."

"Nothing, Mrs. Hampton.
I just dropped my lunch.
He picked it up for me."

"Really? That's great."

21

"Tell Mrs. Hampton what really happened or we will."

"I can't. If I get in trouble again my dad will be really mad."

"It sounds like you've turned over a new leaf."

"I think he has, Mrs. Hampton."

"I'm proud of you."

"Thanks."

Why do you think the boy who was being bullied told the teacher he dropped his lunch?

IMPORTANT IDEAS

On page 8 the bully says, "Yeah, you're just teacher's pet. You always know all the answers."

Why did that make him angry?

What would you do if you saw someone being bullied?

Now that you have read this book, see if you can answer these questions:

1. Why does taking the younger boy's lunch make the older kid a bully?

2. How would working harder make the kid less of a bully?

3. Why does the bully feel he's always in trouble?

4. Do you think the bully has turned over a new leaf? Why or why not?

About the author

Cindy Leaney teaches English and writes books for both young readers and adults. She has lived and worked in England, Kenya, Mexico, Saudi Arabia and the United States.

About the illustrator

Peter Wilks began work in advertising, where he developed a love for illustration. He has drawn pictures for many children's books in Great Britain and in the United States.

HERO CLUB SAFETY SERIES

Do You Smell Smoke? (A Book About Safety with Fire)

Help! I Can't Swim! (A Book About Safety in Water)

Home Sweet Home (A Book About Safety at Home)

Long Walk to School (A Book About Bullying)

Look Out! (A Book About Safety on Bicycles)

Wrong Stop (A Book About Safety from Crime)